KENDRA SMITH

Pocket
Thoughts

A Collection of Poems and Ideas

ISBN: 978-1-4834-5829-8 (sc)
ISBN: 978-1-4834-5828-1 (e)

Lulu Publishing Services rev. date: 01/25/2017

For those who believed me to action.

Contents

Introduction

Welcome to my collection of thoughts to carry with you. Let the ideas, concepts and imaginations brought to you seep deep into the wrinkles of your brain. My hope is to entertain, inspire and provoke you to new thoughts.

Enjoy!

On a Boat

I'm on a boat
Off course
In the storm
Tall waves crash around me
Hungry sharks are in the sea
The wind whips
The rain beats
The water is unforgiving
I sit thinking
With my circumstance
How will I survive?
Then I tell myself
It's a very good thing
My boat is a yacht

Reasons Why
I Must

It takes authority of my being
And crystalizes my seeing

I am able to be my original self
It keeps me off the dusty shelf

It bubbles out the best in me
And make my bones dance with glee

It strikes fear into my darkly doubts
And from my belly it brings great shouts

For life it awakens all my thirst
And make me want to come in first

It creates curiosity for my thoughts
And in life's journey it ties the knots

I can see my future growing
Without the thought of my heart slowing

Reasons why I must

Passion

What is this feeling in the gut of my belly?
It throws me into action
It ignites my emotions
I laugh
I cry
I get excited
My mind is consumed
I am obsessed
Nothing can be done until I have what I desire
My impact will be made
My goal attained
My legacy remembered
This is my passion

Forgotten

I stood alone waiting for you
For I knew our meeting was due
I waited until the sun grew dim
I thought I would go out on a limb
At first I thought you would only be late
So I was open and closed not the gate
I waited until I thought you would come
Then I found this meeting was done

Love Me to Be

I see you walk and pass me by
I stink I smell and I know why
But there is still one thing I need
Love me
Love me to be

Love me to see past my clothes
Give me joy to know a heart that knows
That when I get cut I still bleed
Love me
Love me to be

Your care and compassion goes beyond
Your smile gives hope to carry me on
You planted within a mustard seed
Love me
Love me to be

Now I am able to stand and to live
My heart is open to know and forgive
I can go on and take the lead
Thank you
You loved me to be

My Friend

My dear friend
I give you my heart
Not to the wind of a soul that may part
Only known in seasons
Inner thoughts and reasons
I choose to say
To make your day
And let you in
On my deepest sin
To share in joy and in the pain
The hope of glory in fresh new rain
To see with your eyes and yours with mine
Will make our journey be like wine
The age of true friends is hard to find
I'm so glad that you are mine

Touch

Pat my arm
Relief awakens
I settle
Touch my shoulder
Soul centers
I trust
Hug me
Anxiety abandons
I relax
Touch me

Adversity

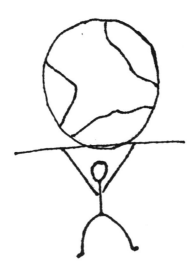

Adversity
My friend
Come closer to me

For you
Make me who
I am really to be

You push, pull
Bind, refine

Because of you
I use my mind

If it weren't for you
I'd be but a babe

In my mother's womb
With not pressure to aid

Adversity
My friend
Come closer to me

For you
Make me who
I am really to be

I Can

I have in life all I need
To be able to succeed

Forward Motion

Step forward today
Momentum make way
I choose
To move
And do what I say

Beauty

Beauty walks and talks with grace
Brings a smile to my face
A blessing to the human race
Full of style and great taste

Impatience

I want it now
I cannot wait
Tell me how
To fix my fate
Too long it takes
For me to find
When I wake
To see what's mine

False Thoughts

I had a thought
It was not true
I found it real
And blamed you
I reacted
To something false
And our friendship
Was the cost

Unnoticed Wisdom

I looked at you
You looked right through me
I said hello
You passed right by
I asked a question
You gave no answer
You didn't even give a sigh
What must it take?
For you to see me
To hear my voice
When I draw nigh
For I have
Your golden answer
If not noticed
I'll say goodbye

Disillusionment

I glanced at you
From that moment
I wanted you

I fanaticized about your
Chocolate icing
Strawberry topping
And cream filling

Day in and day out
I longed for a taste
I couldn't resist

I raced to the bakery
My cake in sight
You will be mine

I shoved money at the clerk
And grabbed you
I sat down quickly
To stare at my bounty

I used a fork
To look civilized
My mouth open
Taste buds waiting

I closed my lips over a morsel
I tasted
And tasted

My lips curved downward
Tears escaped form my eyes
You have coconut flakes
I hate coconut

Calls of Death

My life calls to the grave
Not because I misbehave
But because desired had lied
And said that I already died
Why live why give
To be with Thee
When you have me
As company
Come sleep not weep for eternity
Where you can rest and really be free

Thinking of You

Thinking of you my heart skips a beat
Then I get nervous and look at my feet

I think about love, the difference from lust
What would it be like to live in a trust?

I think about you and think about me
About how together we'd really be free

Free to touch heart and free to explore
Without feeling shame of wanting what's more

What could we make life together as two?
Becoming as one to fit the same shoe

But this is just me just thinking of you
Are you thinking the same of me too?

Sunshine

Warm on my skin
Life to within
Chill chased away
Light to my day

Light

Fear of darkness
Burden of shadows
Destruction of stagnation
Illuminator of truth
Peace of death
Giver of life
Catalyst of change
Awareness of beings
Hope of the ignorant
Wisdom of the knowing

A Whole New
Life Began

I saw her and a whole new life began. I never heard her voice or had the pleasure of holding her hand but I knew one day our lips would touch sealing our devotion to one another.

The trouble is I am extremely shy. I am so shy that I blush at the very thought of her. If I were to be in her presence I think I would faint.

How do I get over myself? I dedicated my life to prayer and meditation. I hoped God would make it easy for me. Maybe sometime soon our destinies would intertwine.

Two weeks went by and she was still admired from afar. I prayed harder, longer and even fasted for three days. Then, the answer came in a dream. This light from heaven came down upon me. A deep voice, but soft, spoke to me. "Go and say hello."

I woke up angry. I expected a miracle. "Go and say hello?" Nonetheless, I was obedient. With sweaty palms and shaky knees I approached her. I said, "Hello." She smiled and a whole new life began.